Kartar Singh Sarabha

This Book Belongs to

Kartar Singh Sarabha was an Indian independence activist and revolutionary who is best known for his role in the Ghadar Movement, a movement that sought to end British colonial rule in India through armed revolt. Sarabha was born in 1895 in the village of Sarabha in the Ludhiana district of Punjab. From a young age, he was deeply interested in politics and social justice, and he became actively involved in the independence movement as a student at the National College in Lahore.

Sarabha is most famous for his role in the Ghadar Movement, which was a group of Indian immigrants to the United States and Canada who sought to foment revolution in India. The group was founded in 1913, and Sarabha became one of its key leaders. He worked tirelessly to recruit new members and to raise funds for the cause, and he played a key role in organizing several armed uprisings in India.

Despite the efforts of the Ghadar Movement, the British were able to suppress the revolts and arrest many of the group's leaders, including Sarabha. In 1916, Sarabha was arrested and charged with sedition. He was sentenced to death, and he was hanged on November 16, 1915, at the age of just 19.

Sarabha's execution did not mark the end of the Ghadar Movement, however. The group continued to operate and to agitate for independence, and it played a key role in the non-violent resistance movement led by Mahatma Gandhi in the 1920s and 1930s. Today, Sarabha is remembered as a hero of the Indian independence movement, and his legacy lives on in the many streets, schools, and other landmarks that bear his name in India and around the world.

Sarabha was born into a Sikh family, and he received a traditional Sikh education. As a young boy, he was deeply influenced by the teachings of the Gurus and the principles of social justice and equality that are at the heart of Sikhism. These values would later inspire him to join the independence movement and to dedicate his life to the cause of freeing India from colonial rule.

Sarabha was an intelligent and ambitious young man, and he excelled academically. He attended the National College in Lahore, where he studied mathematics, physics, and chemistry. It was at this time that he became actively involved in the independence movement, and he quickly rose through the ranks of the Ghadar Party, a group of Indian immigrants in the United States and Canada who were working to end British rule in India.

Sarabha was a natural leader and an eloquent speaker, and he was able to inspire and mobilize many people to join the cause. He worked tirelessly to recruit new members and to raise funds for the Ghadar Party, and he played a key role in organizing several armed uprisings in India. Despite the efforts of the Ghadar Party, the British were able to suppress the revolts and arrest many of the group's leaders, including Sarabha.

Sarabha's execution was a major blow to the independence movement, and it sparked outrage and protests across India. However, his sacrifice did not go in vain, as it inspired many others to continue the fight for independence. The Ghadar Party continued to operate and to agitate for independence, and it played a key role in the non-violent resistance movement led by Mahatma Gandhi in the 1920s and 1930s.

Today, Sarabha is remembered as a hero of the Indian independence movement, and his legacy lives on in the many streets, schools, and other landmarks that bear his name in India and around the world. He is an inspiration to all those who fight for social justice and equality, and his memory serves as a reminder of the sacrifices that have been made in the struggle for freedom. So, these are some lines about Kartar Singh Sarabha.

In addition to his work with the Ghadar Party, Sarabha was also involved in other independence activities. He was a member of the Hindustan Socialist Republican Association (HSRA), a group of Indian revolutionaries who sought to end British rule through armed struggle. Sarabha worked closely with other HSRA leaders, including Bhagat Singh, Sukhdev, and Rajguru, and he played a key role in planning and executing several acts of sabotage against British targets.

Sarabha was arrested several times during his involvement in the independence movement, and he spent a total of three years in prison. Despite the harsh conditions he faced, he remained committed to the cause and never wavered in his belief that India must be freed from colonial rule.

Sarabha's execution at such a young age made him a martyr in the eyes of many, and his sacrifice has been remembered and celebrated by generations of Indians. In 1962, the Government of India posthumously awarded him the Bharat Ratna, the country's highest civilian award, in recognition of his contributions to the independence movement.

Today, Sarabha is remembered as a symbol of resistance and bravery, and his legacy lives on in the hearts and minds of many Indians. His memory serves as a reminder of the sacrifices that were made in the struggle for freedom, and his example continues to inspire people around the world to stand up for their beliefs and to fight for justice and equality. So, these are some more lines about Kartar Singh Sarabha.

After Sarabha's death, the Ghadar Party continued to operate and to agitate for independence, and it played a key role in the non-violent resistance movement led by Mahatma Gandhi in the 1920s and 1930s. The party's efforts, along with those of other independence groups, eventually helped bring about the end of British rule in India in 1947.

In the years since independence, Sarabha's memory has been celebrated and honored in a number of ways. Many streets, schools, and other landmarks in India and around the world bear his name, and his life and legacy are remembered in a number of books, films, and other works of art.

Today, Sarabha is remembered as a hero of the Indian independence movement, and his legacy lives on as an inspiration to all those who fight for social justice and equality. His memory serves as a reminder of the sacrifices that have been made in the struggle for freedom, and his example continues to inspire people around the world to stand up for their beliefs and to fight for a better world. So, these are some additional lines about Kartar Singh Sarabha.

PRACTICE AND NOTES

PRACTICE AND NOTES

PRACTICE AND NOTES

PRACTICE AND NOTES

PRACTICE AND NOTES

PRACTICE AND NOTES

PRACTICE AND NOTES

PRACTICE AND NOTES

PRACTICE AND NOTES

PRACTICE AND NOTES

PRACTICE AND NOTES

PRACTICE AND NOTES

PRACTICE AND NOTES

PRACTICE AND NOTES

PRACTICE AND NOTES

PRACTICE AND NOTES

PRACTICE AND NOTES

PRACTICE AND NOTES

PRACTICE AND NOTES

PRACTICE AND NOTES